Becoming a Grasshopper

by Grace Hansen

Abdo
CHANGING ANIMALS
Kids

abdopublishing.com

Published by Abdo Kids, a division of ABDO, PO Box 398166, Minneapolis, Minnesota 55439.

Printed in the United States of America, North Mankato, Minnesota.

052016

092016

 THIS BOOK CONTAINS RECYCLED MATERIALS

Photo Credits: iStock, Minden Pictures, Science Source, Shutterstock

Production Contributors: Teddy Borth, Jennie Forsberg, Grace Hansen

Design Contributors: Laura Mitchell, Dorothy Toth

Cataloging-in-Publication Data

Names: Hansen, Grace, author.

Title: Becoming a grasshopper / by Grace Hansen.

Description: Minneapolis, MN : Abdo Kids, [2017] | Series: Changing animals |
    Includes bibliographical references and index.

Identifiers: LCCN 2015959113 | ISBN 9781680805109 (lib. bdg.) |
    ISBN 9781680805666 (ebook) | ISBN 9781680806229 (Read-to-me ebook)

Subjects: LCSH: Grasshoppers--Juvenile literature. | Life cycles--Juvenile
    literature.

Classification: DDC 595.7--dc23

LC record available at http://lccn.loc.gov/2015959113

Table of Contents

Stage 1

All grasshoppers begin as eggs. Female grasshoppers lay pods of eggs. Each pod has 20 to 120 eggs. She lays them underground. This keeps them safe.

5

Stage 2

Eggs remain underground for about 10 months. They hatch in the spring or early summer. Newly hatched grasshoppers are called **nymphs**.

A **nymph** looks like an adult grasshopper. But it is very small. It also does not have wings.

9

A **nymph** eats and grows.

It **molts** as it grows.

11

Stage 3

The **nymph** grows for five to six weeks. It is much bigger then. It also has small wings.

The **nymph** has its final **molt**.

It is an adult grasshopper!

14

15

The grasshopper has six strong legs. Its four front legs are for walking. Its two back legs are for jumping!

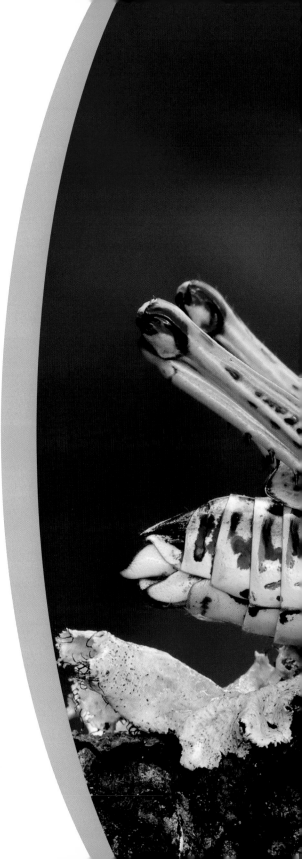

The grasshopper has two antennas. Its antennas are very long.

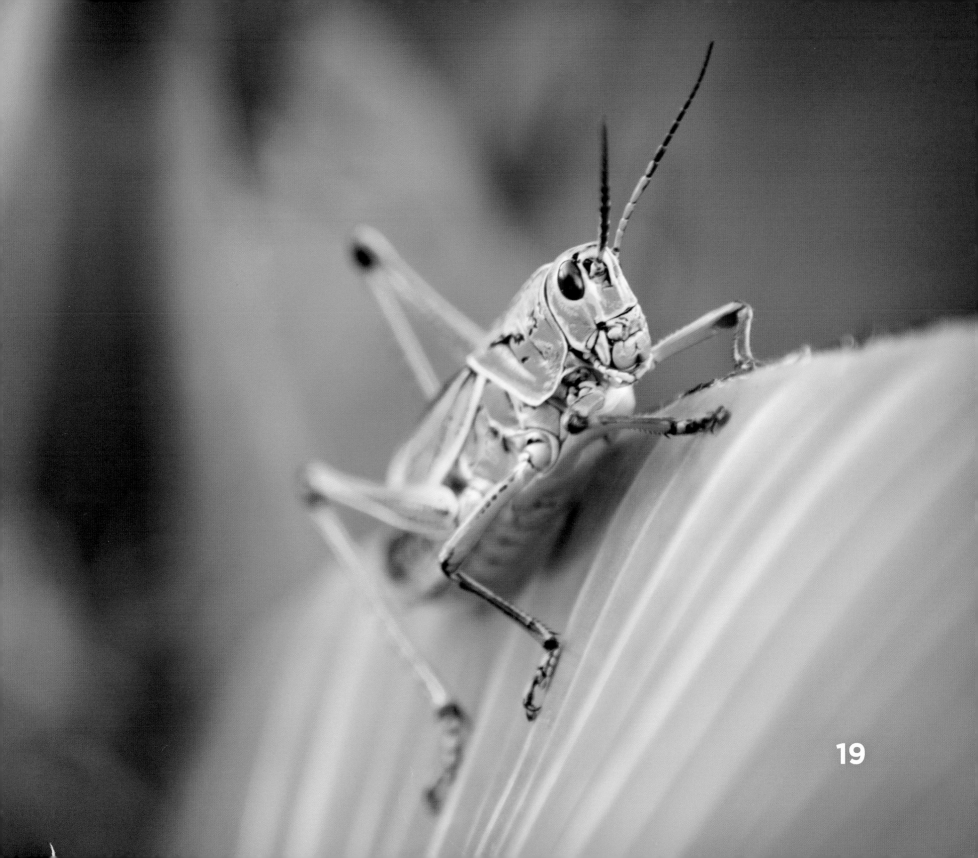

19

The grasshopper will live for about two months. In that time, it will find a **mate**. It will also do lots of eating!

More Facts

- There are more than 11,000 different kinds of grasshoppers in the world.

- Grasshoppers have strong jaws. They are good chewers. Grass is their favorite thing to eat.

- Grasshoppers are amazing jumpers. If humans had the same ability, we would be able to jump the length of a football field!

Glossary

mate – one of a pair of animals that will have young together.

molt – to shed skin that will be replaced by new skin.

nymph – a young insect that has almost the same form as the adult.

Index

abdokids.com

Use this code to log on to abdokids.com and access crafts, games, videos, and more!

Abdo Kids Code:
CBK5109